U0490998

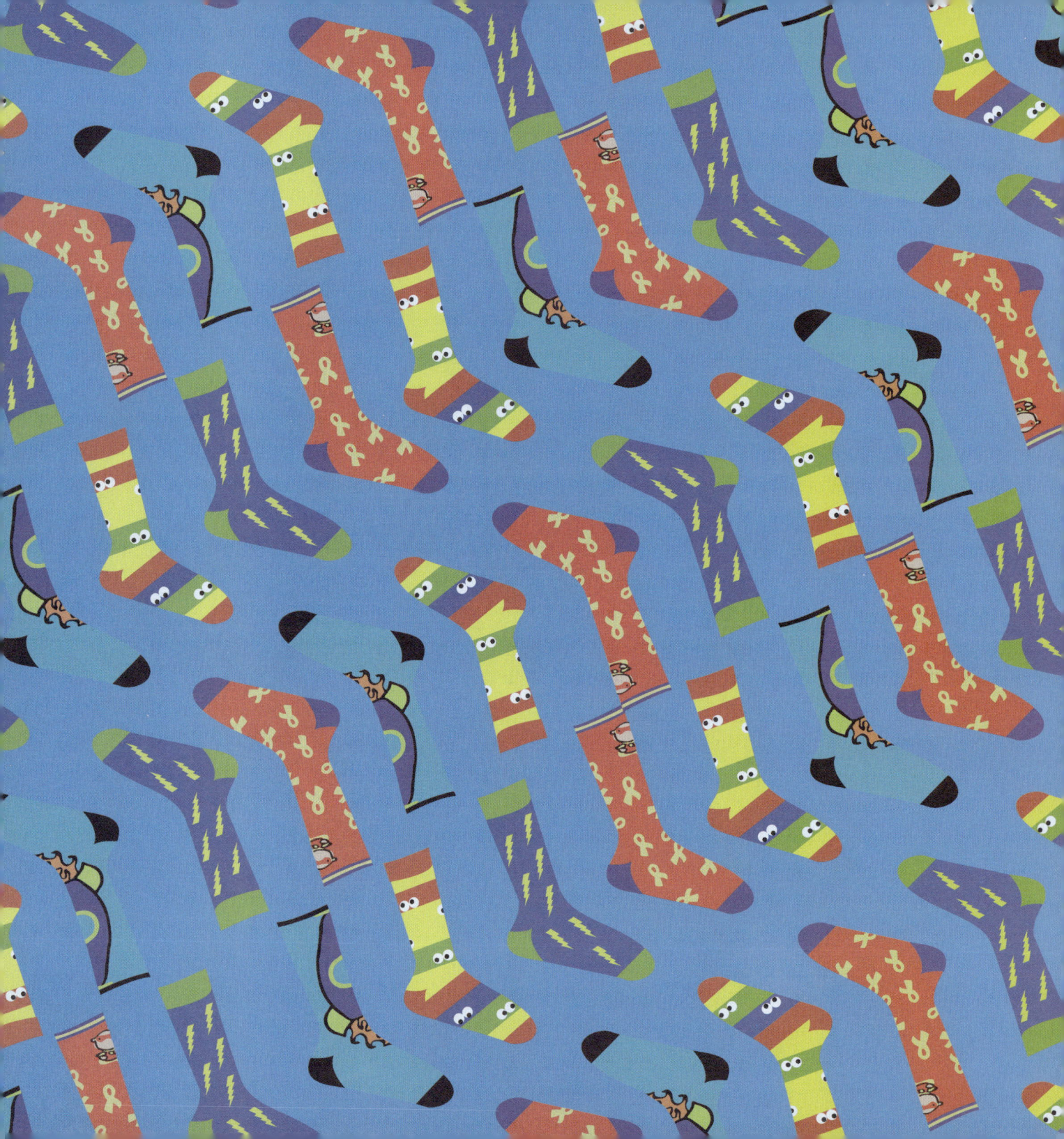

塞巴斯蒂安创造的袜子公司

Sebastian Creates a Sock Company

（汉英对照）

茹燕子（Erica Swallow）著

曾俐 绘/译

张欣 审校

中国财经出版传媒集团

经济科学出版社
Economic Science Press

图书在版编目(CIP)数据

塞巴斯蒂安创造的袜子公司:汉英对照/(美)茹燕子(Erica Swallow)著;曾俐译.—北京:经济科学出版社,2018.12
(创业儿童)
ISBN 978-7-5141-9442-5

Ⅰ.①塞… Ⅱ.①茹…②曾… Ⅲ.①创业-儿童读物-汉、英 Ⅳ.①F241.4-49

中国版本图书馆CIP数据核字(2018)第133369号

塞巴斯蒂安创造的袜子公司(汉英对照)

茹燕子(Erica Swallow) 著
曾 俐 绘/译

责任编辑: 周国强
责任校对: 杨晓莹
责任印制: 邱 天

经济科学出版社出版、发行 新华书店经销
社址:北京市海淀区阜成路甲28号 邮编:100142
电话:总编部 010-88191217 发行部 010-88191522
网址:www.esp.com.cn
邮箱:esp@esp.com.cn
网店:经济科学出版社旗舰店(天猫)
网址:http://jjkxcbs.tmall.com
印刷:中煤(北京)印务有限公司
开本:889×1194 20开 2印张 30000字
版次:2018年12月第1版 2018年12月第1次印刷
书号:ISBN 978-7-5141-9442-5
定价:48.00元

(图书出现印装问题,本社负责调换。电话:010-88191510)
(版权所有 侵权必究 打击盗版 举报热线:010-88191661
QQ:2242791300 营销中心电话:010-88191537
电子邮箱:dbts@esp.com.cn)

塞巴斯蒂安·马丁内斯(小塞)酷爱袜子,他收藏的袜子五颜六色,令人着迷。

Sebastian Martinez had the most colorful, crazy sock collection of anyone around.

那是我弟弟。他超级喜欢袜子!
That's my little brother. He loooooooves socks!

圆点袜、条纹袜、锯齿袜、漩涡花纹袜……任何你能想到的款式,他都有。

Polka dots, stripes, zigzags, and swirly swoops, he had every kind of sock you could imagine.

从小到大，无论小塞去哪儿都会穿着他那些稀奇古怪的袜子。

Growing up, Sebastian wore his wacky socks everywhere.

去学校……

To school...

下泳池……

To the pool...

篮球训练时，其他小孩都穿着单调无趣的黑袜子，小塞却不一样。

And even to basketball practice, where all the other kids wore boring black socks.

无论走到哪儿，小塞都被称作"袜子男孩儿"。

Everywhere he went, Sebastian was known as the Sock Kid.

一天，小塞被叫到了校长办公室。

"你可不能再穿那些古怪的袜子了，"校长晃着手指说："这违反了校服规定！"

One day at school, Sebastian got called to the principal's office.

"You can't wear wacky socks anymore," the principal said, waving her finger. "It's against the uniform policy!"

小塞不知如何是好。他太爱那些袜子了，如果平日不能穿去学校，简直无法想象！

Sebastian didn't know how to react. He loved his socks so much and couldn't imagine a day without them.

回到家里,小塞的家人都陪着他,让他感到自己很特别。

Back at home, Sebastian's family made him feel really special for the rest of the day.

煎饼,你的最爱!
Pancakes, your favorite!

今天你说了算!
King for the day!

吃完晚饭我们一起去打球吧!
Let's shoot some hoops after dinner!

有了家人的鼓舞,小塞心情好多了。

Sebastian felt better knowing his family was there to cheer him up.

小塞不能再穿着有趣的袜子去学校了，但他把袜子装在了书包里，这样一放学他就能立刻换上袜子了。真是个聪明的孩子！

Sebastian couldn't wear his fun socks to school anymore, but he kept them in his backpack, so he could put them on as soon as class ended. He was a clever kid!

见到儿子对袜子如此着迷，小塞妈妈有了个主意。她说："你既然这么喜欢袜子，为何不自己设计呢？"

Seeing how much Sebastian loved socks, his mom had an idea. "You love socks so much," she said. "Why don't you design your own?"

"这点子太棒了!"小塞大声赞叹道,他立马抓起了纸和马克笔,飞奔去了餐桌。

"What a great idea!" Sebastian shouted, running to the kitchen table with paper and markers in hand.

赞!赞!赞!
Yes! Yes! Yes!

小塞开始画他脑海中的袜子。开心的袜子、悲伤的袜子、有趣的袜子、疯狂的袜子,他都一一画了出来。

He started drawing all the socks he had ever dreamed of. Happy socks, sad socks, funny socks, and mad socks, he drew them all.

画了几个小时之后，小塞向妈妈展示了他最喜欢的一张。"您能给它们打个洞么?这样我就能穿了。"他问道。

After hours of drawing, Sebastian presented his favorite picture. "Can you put a hole in it, so I can wear it?" he asked.

妈妈笑道：" 袜子真好看！但我们得用别的材料才能做成真的可以穿的那种袜子。"

His mom laughed. "Nice sock! But we're going to have to use different supplies if you want to create a real sock that you can wear."

小塞的妈妈下定决心帮助儿子实现梦想。她联系了很多朋友,终于有一天,她找到了一家工厂,他们可以把小塞画的袜子变成真袜子!

Sebastian's mom was determined to help make her son's dream a reality. She called friends everywhere, until one day, she found a factory that could help turn Sebastian's drawings into real socks!

他们给工厂发了许多设计图。

They sent many designs to the factory.

他们等啊等啊,终于收到了真的袜子!

After a long wait, real socks arrived by mail!

"在工厂批量生产这些袜子之前,你还有没有想修改的地方?"爸爸问道。

"Is there anything you'd change about this sock before the factory makes more?" Sebastian's dad asked.

"这款袜子真是帅呆了、酷毙了、堪称完美！"小塞抱着袜子赞叹道，"我觉得一定会有更多的人喜欢这些袜子。"

"This sock is awesomely, amazingly, stupendously perfect!" Sebastian shouted, hugging it. "I think more people would love to have socks like these."

就这样，小塞的袜子公司诞生了！

That is how Sebastian's sock company was born.

小塞的哥哥布莱登也来帮忙了。接下来的几个月，兄弟俩给工厂发去了更多的袜子图样。一天，他们收到了成箱的袜子，简直堆成了小山！

Sebastian's older brother, Brandon, started helping out. As the months went by, the boys sent many more sock patterns to the factory. One day, a mountain of boxes arrived!

!!!

你们觉得有多少箱？
How many boxes do you think we have?

至少104箱！
At least 104!

天啊，我们都能搭一个城堡了！
Holy moly, we could build a castle!

小塞和布莱登在当地一家鞋店外搭了一个小摊，想看看到底有没有人会买他们的袜子。

鞋店经理也乐意把一张靠门的桌子给他们用。

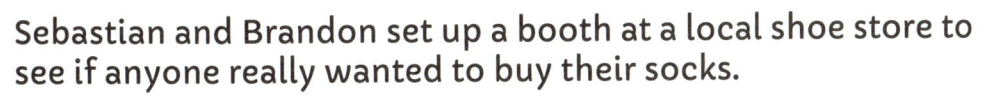

Sebastian and Brandon set up a booth at a local shoe store to see if anyone really wanted to buy their socks.

The store manager happily gave them a table right by the door.

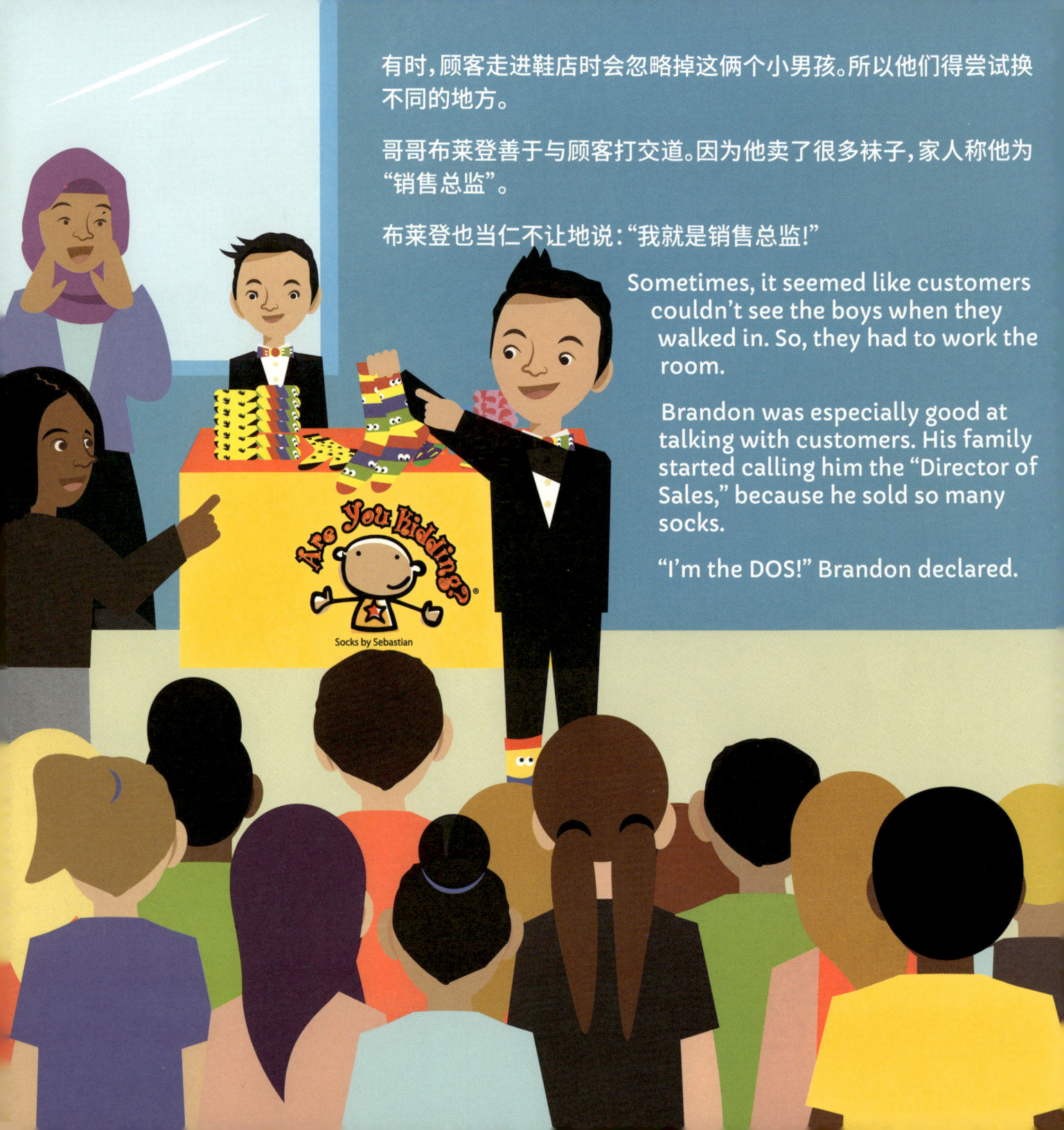

有时，顾客走进鞋店时会忽略掉这俩个小男孩。所以他们得尝试换不同的地方。

哥哥布莱登善于与顾客打交道。因为他卖了很多袜子，家人称他为"销售总监"。

布莱登也当仁不让地说："我就是销售总监！"

Sometimes, it seemed like customers couldn't see the boys when they walked in. So, they had to work the room.

Brandon was especially good at talking with customers. His family started calling him the "Director of Sales," because he sold so many socks.

"I'm the DOS!" Brandon declared.

年龄最小的 CEO
塞巴斯蒂安

那晚,小塞梦到了他的新公司。他从来没见过其他小孩开公司,那他是世界上年纪最小的首席执行官吗?

Later that night, Sebastian dreamed about his new business. He had never seen other kids run businesses. Was he the youngest CEO in the world?

一年过去了,小塞也明白了创业不会凡事都一帆风顺。

After a year in business, Sebastian learned that sometimes there are hard days.

盈利
Sales
$

比如他费尽心思做出来的袜子设计,结果无人问津……

Like when nobody buys your favorite sock design, even though you worked really hard on it...

或者不小心被客厅讨厌的盒子绊倒,摔伤膝盖……

Or you trip over one of those pesky boxes in the living room and hurt your knee...

再比如整周都想不出好的袜子创意!
Or you run out of sock design ideas for a whole week!

风雨过去总有彩虹，兄弟俩的付出也终于得到了收获。

But there are also great days that make up for all the rough times.

比如他们都被邀请上过电视。
Sebastian and Brandon have been on aTV.

捐款 Donation

他们也捐了很多钱给不同的慈善机构。
They've given lots of money to many charities.

有一次还见到了当地消防英雄，兄弟俩因创业与捐赠的善举也被授予"荣誉消防员"的称号。
They once met a local hero at the fire department, who made them honorary firefighters for all of the good work they do.

特殊袜子日
Special Socks Day!

学校还为他们特设了"袜子日",
允许所有学生在那天穿上各式奇异的袜子上学!

And they finally got their school to let them wear funky socks on special days!

小塞的创业始于他梦想做出自己的袜子。如今，不论老少，大家都穿着他设计的奇异的袜子。

Sebastian's business all began with a dream to make his own socks, and now people everywhere, of all ages, wear his wacky creations.

在家人、朋友和社区的帮助下，他实现了自己的梦想。

With the help of his family, friends, and the community around him, he brought his dreams to life.

如果你是一个有雄心的小小创业者，小塞想给你一点儿特别的建议……

"无论5岁还是70岁，任何年纪、任何时候你都可以开始创业。"别让任何人阻挡你追求梦想的脚步！

If you're an aspiring Entrepreneur Kid, Sebastian has a special message for you...

"You're never too young or too old to start a business. You can be 5 or 70." Don't let anyone get in the way of your dreams!

别让任何人阻挡你追求梦想的脚步
Don't let anyone get in the way of your dreams!

现在轮到你了……你想为这个世界解决什么问题呢？

Now it's your turn... What problems do you want to solve in the world?

作者寄语

《塞巴斯蒂安创造的袜子公司》讲述了"创业家"塞巴斯蒂安·马丁内斯(小塞)五岁时在家人的帮助下创办袜子公司"你在逗我玩?"的故事。小塞同学热衷于穿各种各样的奇怪袜子,在上学前班的时候就被大伙称之为"袜子男孩儿"。小塞的祖母在百货商店工作,每次去看望他时都会捎上袜子。与其他孩子不同,小塞很喜欢祖母带给他的袜子,在五岁的时候就已经收集了超过100双色彩斑斓款式独特的长袜。小塞的妈妈瑞秋·马丁内斯于是鼓励他:"为什么你不试试自己设计袜子呢?"她仍然清楚地记得这一天是2013年6月25日。

妈妈的询问激起了小塞的斗志,并标志着小塞袜子生意的开始,从这一天起小塞进入了设计袜子的全速战斗状态。在妈妈的帮助下,小塞的袜子设计梦想最终变成了现实。作为广告出版主管,妈妈瑞秋在拉丁美洲有很广的人脉关系。她立刻投入工作,思考怎样才能让儿子的袜子设计成为实物。最终她联系到一家位于危地马拉的制造商生产样品。

2014年5月,"你在逗我玩?"成为了一家真正的公司,6岁的塞巴斯蒂安·马丁内斯当起了CEO,妈妈瑞秋任总裁。同年6月袜子到货时,马丁内斯和亲戚家都堆满了装货的箱子,准备开始出售。

哥哥布莱登出色的社交能力在公司开业的第一天就大放异彩。小塞和妈妈在佛罗里达州迈阿密"芝麻步童鞋"店的门口支起了一张小桌。小塞一开始显得非常害羞,不敢同陌生人说话。于是妈妈打电话给爸爸法比安,让他带哥哥布莱登过来,给"你在逗我玩?"注入一些活力。这个方法果然有效,布莱登一到,顾客就争先恐后地来抢购小塞的袜子。

塞巴斯蒂安和布莱登两兄弟在设计袜子。摄影:瑞秋·马丁内斯(Rachel Martinez)

那日,布莱登获得了"销售总监"头衔,按他自己的话说是"管家"。公司一早就迎来了第一笔单子,布莱登的正能量也带动了顾客的兴趣。同时,他的自信和销售才能也给弟弟小塞树立了一个好榜样。

如今,兄弟俩不仅拥有一家销量数以万计的袜子公司,同时也与多家非营利慈善组织合作,销售定制设计的袜子,以此支持许多机构的工作——比如"活得像贝拉基金会"、"打败渐冻人症"、"自闭症之声"、"布丽娜·维加拉基金"以及"美国癌症协会"。

由于在为提高儿科癌症关注度和慈善方面有着杰出的贡献,小塞和哥哥被迈阿密市长授予了特殊表彰,这也是兄弟俩得到的荣誉中最让他们骄傲的一个。与此同时,他们被迈阿密消防救援联盟授予了"荣誉消防员"的称号,因此而获得的乘坐直升机的奖励更让兄弟俩津津乐道。兄弟俩出现在很多的主流媒体上:诸如"早安美国"、"哈里秀"、"Univision西班牙语晚间新闻"和"CNN西班牙语频道"的大银幕上,他们的故事也持续激励着很多人。

"你在逗我玩?"公司除了售卖包括瓢虫、泡泡、火箭、瞪眼(小塞的最爱)等一系列儿童和成人款的袜子之外,也有各种为慈善组织定制的袜子。

我和插画师曾俐、摄影师丹·东贝在写这部书的时候拜访了小塞和马丁内斯一家。本书的故事和图片取材于与小塞及其家人的面谈及网上访谈。想要了解更多关于小塞、布莱登和"你在逗我玩?"公司的故事请访问:entrepreneurkid.com和areyoukidding.net,里面有详细的视频、图片和图书等信息。

马丁内斯一家在2016年贝拉舞会。摄影:耶塞妮娅·冈萨雷斯 (Yesenia Gonzalez)

"你在逗我玩?"袜子。摄影:瑞秋·马丁内斯 (Rachel Martinez)

你读过多少《创业儿童》的丛书？

《创业儿童》系列共有四本书。通读全四册，了解其他孩子是如何开始创业的。通过解决生活中的问题，你也可以成为创业儿童。

How many Entrepreneur Kid books have you read?

There are four books in the Entrepreneur Kid series. Read them all to learn how other kids like you started their own businesses. You, too, can be an Entrepreneur Kid by solving problems around you.

扫码关注创作者

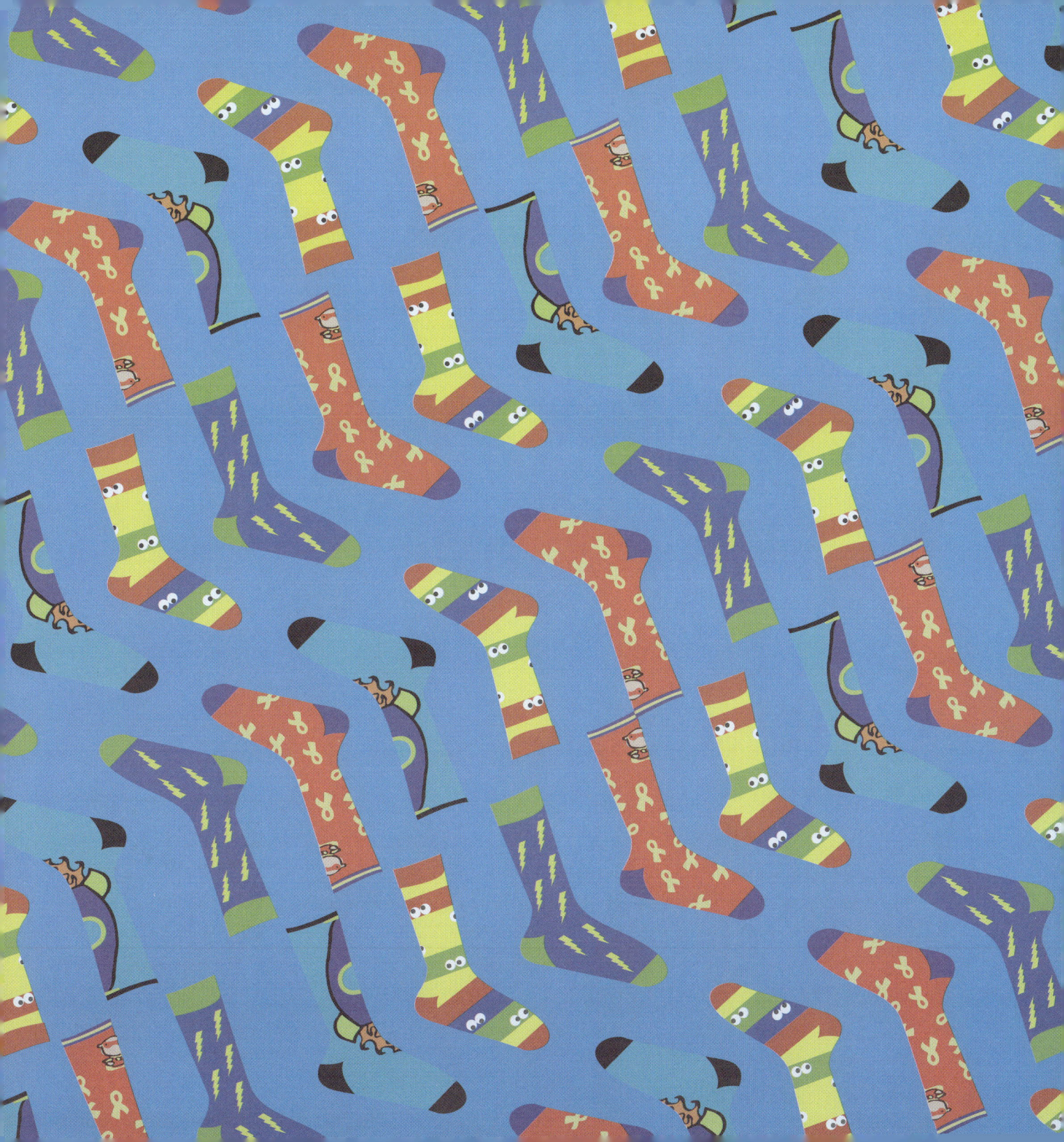

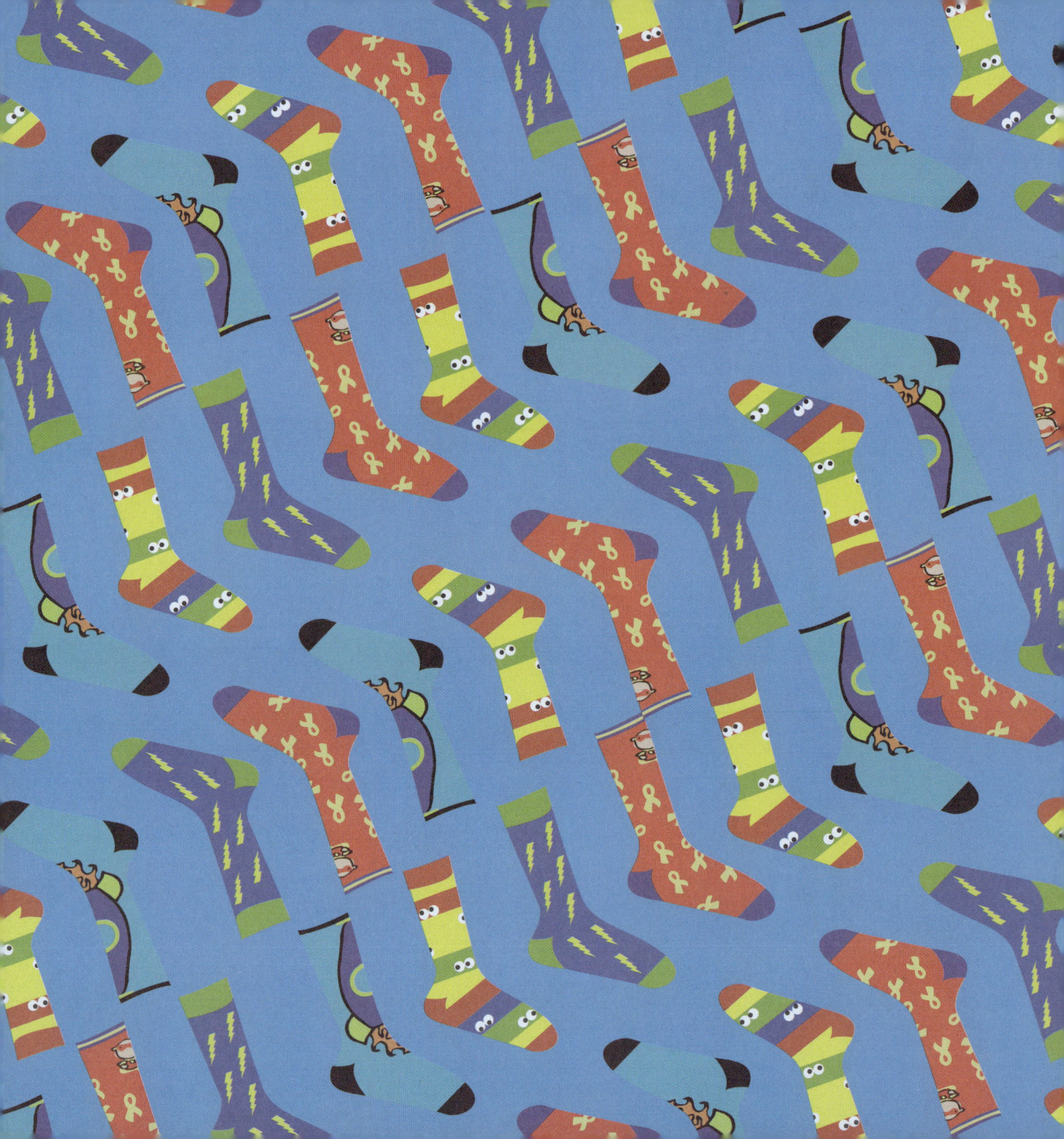